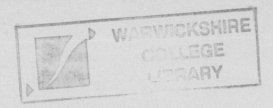

Small Books on Great Gardens

NINFA

A Roman Enchantment

Lauro Marchetti and Esme Howard

Photography by Claire de Virieu

Contents

An Overview

The internationally renowned garden of Ninfa is situated some forty-five miles (seventy kilometers) southeast of Rome and fifteen miles (twenty-five kilometers) from the sea in the province of Lazio. The garden was laid out in the 1920s among the ruins of the small medieval town of Ninfa, which was founded in the eighth century and destroyed by the inhabitants of hostile neighboring towns in 1381.

For most of its history Ninfa and the surrounding land have been the property of the venerable Caetani family. The town itself was built at the foot of the Lepini Mountains next to a small lake fed by springs of ice-cold water. The building of the town and, much later, the creation of the garden in that place were motivated largely by the abundance and purity of the waters, which have not only inspired poets and artists,

For captions of previous illustrations, see page 80. The alluring arch, *opposite*, leads to an enclosed garden. *Above*, the decorative pattern on the stone is based on the Caetani coat of arms.

Opposite: Reflections of a Judas tree in the clear, limpid water of the river. *Overleaf*: Morning light on the river below the Ponte Romano.

but from as early as the eighth century were recognized for their economic and strategic potential.

Ninfa is exposed to the south but protected from the north by the mountains. It thus avoids the cold northerly winds, while capturing and storing in its hard limestone rocks the incoming warmth of the Mediterranean. Visitors are often surprised to find a garden so green, luxuriant, and full of life in so dry a climate, but it is this combination of favorable weather, abundant water, and the creative genius of man over the centuries, that makes Ninfa unique.

The earth at Ninfa is rich, well drained, moist, and alkaline–conditions that make plants grow rapidly. The hot summer temperatures and moisture also permit rapid acclimatization of a wide variety of such tropical and other plants from extreme climates as the Arolla pine from the high mountains of the Alps and the Casuarina from Madagascar.

The garden was conceived and developed by the last three generations of the Caetani family and is now one of several country properties owned and administered by the Fondazione Roffredo Caetani. It is loved and admired by thousands of people from all over the world, not only for its singular atmosphere but also as a paradigm of conservation and protection. The strict rules laid down for public visits have made it possible to

Previous pages: Spring patterns provide a dramatic and colorful contrast to the ruined buildings and monuments of a once thriving township.

Right: A pathway leading to the Ponte di Legno (wooden bridge).

Opposite: Pietro Caetani's fortified tower completed in 1300 and, below it, the Villa Caetani, once Ninfa's Palazzo Comunale, or town hall. The cypress tree was one of many planted in the 1920s. In the foreground a clump of *Gunnera manicata*.

conserve not only the harmony and integrity of the whole garden but also the traditional values bequeathed to it by the last Caetani owners.

In the running of the garden today, as always, much attention is given to the balance between flora and fauna, between water, historic monuments, and man himself. To achieve this it has always been necessary to reduce to a minimum any unnatural interference with the environment of Ninfa and its surrounding properties. The result is a blend of the cultivated and the wild, of the romantic and the rational, and above all a lasting sensation of the mysterious and the sacred.

History of Ninfa
and the
Caetani Family

The name Ninfa comes from a little temple built near the spring and dedicated to nymph goddesses in Roman times. Here, Pliny the Elder found inspiration for his poetry and travellers would stop to refresh themselves. In 750 the estates of Ninfa and Norma were acquired by Pope Zacharias, who wanted them not just for their proximity to Rome but also to amplify Church properties and make maximum economic use of them. By that time the estates were vast, stretching from the slopes of the mountains to the sea.

In the eighth century agricultural production in the area was taxed, and it is believed Ninfa became a center for regional organization and administration. During the ninth and tenth centuries it was a frequent stopping point for travellers making their way along the Via Piedemontana between Rome and Naples when the Via

Opposite: The ruined archway leading into the nave of Santa Maria Maggiore, the finest of Ninfa's seven church monuments, where Rolando Bandinelli was crowned Pope Alexander III in 1159.

Overleaf: The brilliant early sunshine at Ninfa, breaking over the mountain, creates strong contrasts of light and shade.

Opposite: The exquisite little waterfalls designed by Duke Roffredo and his American-born wife Marguerite Chapin. These and other subsidiary watercourses flow directly from the lake, eventually joining the main river in powerful cascades.
Overleaf: A maple tree (Acer palmatum) growing happily in the sheltering walls of a typical Ninfa dwelling of the twelfth century.

Appia was flooded by the Pontine Marshes. Tolls were routinely levied.

The fortified structure of the town of Ninfa was developed by the various popes of the eleventh century, who were anxious to control the properties and the strategic position. The whole area was richly agricultural and generously supplied with water. At the beginning of the twelfth century Ninfa was more populous than neighboring fortified towns. For several decades it did, however, suffer from the general decline in the Lazio region, and successive pontiffs made land concessions to a number of powerful families in return for money. In 1159 Rolando Bandinelli was crowned Alexander III in the church of Santa Maria Maggiore at Ninfa, whose ruins stand tall to this day.

Sadly, few records documenting life at Ninfa then exist today, but the surviving architecture and frescoes of its seven churches, as well as the fortifications, make it clear that by the end of the century Ninfa had reached a high point in architectural and artistic accomplishment, in commerce, and in military prestige.

In 1213, shortly after the coronation of Innocent III, Ninfa passed to a member of the powerful Conti family, who remained concessionaires for several decades until Cardinal Pietro Colonna gained the fiefdom in 1293 with the support of the Annibaldi. Pope Boniface VIII, a

bitter opponent of the Colonna family, bought Ninfa in 1297 for two hundred thousand gold florins and gave it to his nephew Pietro Caetani. With the help of his powerful uncle, Pietro Caetani worked assiduously to improve administration, establishing rules to empower the family still more and to back up their entitlements within a solid legal framework.

Opposite: Two pines (*Pinus pinea*) stand guard on each side of the arched gateway to the hortus conclusus.

Left: Part of the beautiful rock garden, so much loved by Donna Lelia, adjacent to the remains of San Biagio. The rocks and stones themselves were taken from the outer walls of Ninfa, breached for the last time in 1382.

Overleaf: The last stretch of the River Ninfa before it leaves the garden, flowing under the double arches of the Ponte del Macello and out into the nature reserve surrounding Ninfa. It reaches the sea some fifteen miles (twenty-five kilometers) away.

29

With the Caetani family fully in control, Ninfa underwent a profound change that proved economically and commercially beneficial to the population. Farming was given great importance, particularly grain, vegetables, and meat. Other income was derived from fish caught in the river Ninfa and in surrounding canals, and from the cultivation of vineyards. The Caetanis also encouraged the growth of small industries, building various mills at Ninfa to produce flour and oil, and also a tannery for the

Opposite: Gelasio Caetani made his studio in this riverside house, where he often worked late into the night by the light of oil. *Overleaf*: Clusters of roses, arum lilies, and aquatic irises compete to adorn a stream that irrigates the outer areas of the garden.

processing of hides. These initiatives were made possible by damming the lake just above the town and passing the water through sluices to drive rudimentary machinery. Today there is an echo of this system in the running of hydroelectric turbines at the head of the river. The abundant water flowing through the town and between the houses also enabled the inhabitants to cultivate many small gardens, turning Ninfa into an oasis, a foresight of how it would look some seven hundred years later.

Under the Caetani family, Ninfa underwent a period of rapid expansion during the thirteenth and fourteenth centuries. At its peak, Ninfa had an imposing double perimeter wall punctuated by fortified watchtowers protecting seven churches, approximately 150 houses, fourteen towers, a castle, a town hall, various mills, and about two thousand inhabitants.

This period of prosperity ended during the civil wars provoked by the Great Schism of the Roman Catholic Church. Ninfa fell to mercenary troops from Brittany and the Basque country, among others, in 1381, during the pontificate of the anti-pope, the so-called Clement VII, who was the challenger to Pope Urban VI and an adversary of the Caetani. Bands from neighboring areas ultimately destroyed Ninfa, and the community ceased to exist. The inhabitants fled in disarray, resettling

eventually in Sermoneta and other neighboring towns and villages.

For several decades local farmers continued to use the water and the mills, and to quarry for stone. But successive generations of the former inhabitants were afraid of the ruined town, the legendary scene of so much violence and desolation. Later efforts to resettle were frustrated by a strong outbreak of malaria in the region, followed by a radical social and economic deterioration in the area that lasted until quite recently. Ninfa's destiny for six centuries, even though the property remained a Caetani fiefdom, was to be one of silence and oblivion.

Two interesting developments occured between the destruction of Ninfa and the present day. An iron foundry built next to the main water source in 1470 enjoyed some commercial success. In the 1600s Francesco Caetani created a brilliantly conceived formal garden in an area protected by the old walls of the town. This Italianate garden was crossed by hedges and planted with a great quantity of bulbs, particularly tulips. Francesco Caetani was highly cultured and a passionate horticulturist, as well as being both viceroy of the two Sicilies and governor of Milan. As with the Caetanis of the twelfth and twentieth centuries, Francesco was the Renaissance embodiment of the genius for gardening present in this illustrious family.

Opposite: Water is accessible throughout the gardens, not only from delightful streams such as this, but also from man-made canals and a centrally controlled system of underground ducts. All the water flows directly from the lake, which is higher than the garden itself.

37

The Garden and the
Last Caetani Owners

From the time of Pietro Caetani, Ninfa and its territories remained in the Caetani family in an extraordinary succession that ultimately revived the fortunes of Ninfa, transforming it from a place of desolation and melancholy to one bursting with life once more.

We pick up the story at the beginning of this century. Times may have changed but not the Caetani family, which, boasting popes, cardinals, political leaders, and men of rare cultivation, continued to exemplify outstanding gifts and qualities and distinguish itself with achievements fit for posterity.

It was Prince Gelasio Caetani who began the restoration and environmental recovery of the forgotten town. This patient architect, writer, and soldier was ahead of his time in techniques of restoration and

Opposite: The angular branches of a maple (*Acer palmatum* 'Dissectum Rubrum').
Overleaf: *Magnolia x soulangiana* hangs over one of the ornamental ponds.

Right: The hedgehog is
one of fifteen species of
mammal residing at Ninfa.
Opposite: Umbrella pines
(*Pinus pinea*) towering
over the bamboo
plantation.

42

ecology. With his English mother Ada Bootle
Wilbraham, the first of the three celebrated Caetani
duchesses to be involved with Ninfa, he cleared the
overgrown ruins of the old town and made the original
plantings of the tall trees we see today. Gelasio
excavated and restored the ancient ruins of houses and
churches, using experience gained in his restoration of

another major Caetani property, the castle of Sermoneta
about three miles (five kilometers) to the south. He also
undertook the enormous task of writing *Domus
Caetana*, the history of the family and its links over
twenty centuries to this part of Italy.

   After centuries of neglect Ninfa was described in
1860 by German historian Gregorovius as "the Pompeii
of the Middle Ages." With just a few trees left and a
thick mantle of vegetation covering the ruins, the

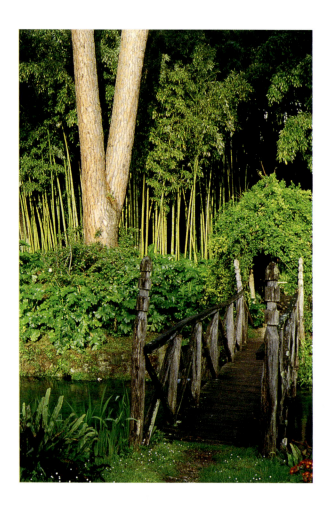

Right: The Ponte di Legno, a favorite observation and resting point for visitors, weas built in 1947 and most recently restored in 1998.
Opposite: The magnificent bamboo (*Phyllostachys mitis*) planted by Ada and Gelasio Caetani in the 1920s, is watered by the purest of all Ninfa's independent springs.

transformation of the ruined town into a romantic garden required imagination bordering on genius.

As work proceeded in clearing the site and bringing the waters under control once more, it became obvious that the emerging garden needed to become part of its natural setting, complementing rather than dominating the historic ruins. This meant a predominantly free and informal style and layout, with little hint of geometric restraint except in the cypress avenues that follow the lines of the ancient streets.

The garden was brought into being with such principles in mind, Donna Ada giving it a distinctly Anglo-Saxon influence. She was no newcomer to garden design, and twenty years earlier had created a fine garden at the family seaside property at Fogliano. She was expert in the adaptation of plants to new climates, and imported and cultivated many varieties there. A fine horsewoman, she reveled in the Pontine countryside. Unfortunately the estate was incompetently managed after her time and was virtually abandoned. Fogliano had all the makings of one of the great nature reserves of Italy, situated as it is inside the Circeo National Park next to some of the finest dunes and beaches in the country.

The principal restoration and recovery work at Ninfa lasted from the twenties until the early fifties, giving us

47

a clear indication of their magnitude. The river was dried out on several occasions to allow the banks to be built up and the bridges strengthened. The 105-foot (thirty-two meter) castle tower was completely renovated, and most of the churches restored along with the old town hall building, later to become the Caetani's country residence. Several fourteenth-century houses were made habitable for the gardeners and their families.

48

Right: This section of the river bank is backed by an imposing curtain of bamboo.
Opposite: Above all, Ninfa is animated by water, which creates its own often-changing micro-environment for flora of all kinds in this case acquatic iris and *Gunnera manicata*.

Along the line of the ancient street of Ninfa, Gelasio planted numerous cypresses (*Cupressus sempervirens*) the most notable of which are along the Via del Ponte. He also planted cedars (Atlantic and Lebanese) and American walnut (*Juglans nigra*), which he is believed to have introduced while serving as Italian Ambassador to Washington.

The great work continued under Marguerite Caetani, née Chapin, the American-born wife of Duke Roffredo, who had by now inherited the estate from his older brother. Marguerite founded and directed two

outstanding literary reviews, in which appeared some of the most important writers of that generation. After living in Paris for many years she moved permanently to Rome and became increasingly immersed in the work at Ninfa, expanding and nurturing the garden with great skill and making it a center of inspiration for poets and artists. She planted many of the big magnolias and roses we see today. With her husband Roffredo she designed the distinctive watercourses and waterfalls. Their son Camillo, the last male heir to Ninfa, died tragically during the World War II.

Opposite: The three romantic essentials of Ninfa–water, plant life, and ruin-are well represented here.
Below: Many of the ruined houses at Ninfa are garlanded with roses.
Overleaf: The rock garden sloping down into the

51

Piazzale della Gloria. The abundant planting includes verbenas, hebes, salvias, alyssum, annual escholtzias, and miniature pomegranates.

Thus Ninfa passed to Camillo's sister Donna Lelia, the last of this ancient family, for whom it was to become a consuming passion. In 1951 she married Hubert Howard, himself a member of the Anglo-Italian nobility, who dedicated himself to the administration of the Caetani estates. Lelia is primarily responsible for the appearance of the garden today, but with no loss of the original inspiration and sense of tradition. As a

Previous pages: Ninfa shows the spectacular relationship among inspirational planting, good husbandry, and the unique and elegant setting of the ancient town.

Right: Six different varieties of ornamental cherry give long periods of color in the Piazzale della Gloria, one of the most exposed areas of the garden.

Opposite: The basic maintenance of each stone monument, in relation to its surrounding plant life, lies with successive generations of gardeners at Ninfa.

gifted painter she often used her artistic imagination to position trees and plants, always considering color, form, and continuity throughout the seasons. Before her premature death in 1977, Lelia created two foundations to which she left the entire family estate, including Ninfa, the castle of Sermoneta, the farms, and the Palazzo Caetani in Rome, which houses one of the most

important historical archives in Rome. Hubert Howard became first president of the foundations created by Lelia to own and to manage Ninfa. He died in 1987.

The history of the garden is, then, the history of three extraordinary women who, in a period of seven decades, transformed a wilderness into a resplendent work of art that is now respected, admired, and loved the world over.

Ninfa does not conform to any specific design or horticultural program. From the beginning spontaneity has been the key, giving visitors the impression of minimal human intervention. Plants are not cultivated unless really necessary, and this factor contributes towards the garden's sense of freedom. Care and husbandry follow the principle of controlled disorder and yet every single plant growing in a ruined building or a hedge, or peeping from a medieval window, is known and cared for. Ninfa cannot be managed along conventional or predictable lines.

Plant care, as Donna Lelia practiced it, was almost secondary to the pursuit of artistic harmony–of greens in the setting of ruins, of colors against stone, and of detail in relation to views and horizons. Visitors often

Opposite: Flowering cherry trees punctuate the lengthy lavender avenue as it crosses the Piazzale della Gloria. *Above*: Francesco Caetani built this classical Renaissance fountain early in the seventeenth century.

speak of Ninfa's sense of mystery. In spite of its breathtaking beauty and horticultural accomplishment, it is the experience of walking through Ninfa that lingers in the memory, even more than the individual highlights.

The garden is not divided into sections, but consists of contrasting moods, sometimes unexpected, at times familiar, but always pleasurable. The different stages in Ninfa's planting history help to explain this. Ada, who started work on the garden in the twenties, planted the tall trees that today provide such a contrast to the majestic ruins of the town and afford shelter to so many plant varieties. Marguerite continued with bright shrub plantings, particularly *Prunus*, *Malus*, and roses, while her daughter Lelia was responsible for the majority of the plants seen today, from climbing rose varieties to shrubs and herbs. She also planted trees just outside the garden boundaries, creating a small arboretum.

Entering the garden from the castle precinct, one is immediately attracted by the sound of racing water from the lake above. In this area are many magnolias including *Magnolia denudata*, M. *Sargentiana*, M. *Sprengeri*, M. *Stellata Rosea*, M. *Campbellii*, M. x *Loeben liebneri*, *Soulengiana 'Lennei*,' and nearby in the birch grove is the large-leafed Rodgersia, so rarely found in this climate.

In front of three large copper beeches around the

Above: Ceanothus arboreus, one of Ninfa's five
spectacular varieties, at Santa Maria Maggiore.
Opposite: In parts of the gardens daisies are allowed
to grow spontaneously in early spring.

church of Santa Maria Maggiore are flowering cherries *Prunus incisa* and P. x *hillieri.* The lively colors of the flowering cherries make them visible all over the garden, and in certain areas, such as the comparatively open Piazzale della Gloria, there are significant concentrations of them (*'Shirotae,' 'Taihaku,' 'Ukon,'* *P. subhirtella 'Pendula'*). Donna Lelia loved dogwood (*Cornus*), which she planted in the more elevated parts of the garden (*C. Capitata, C. Controversa, C. Kousa, C. Florida*).

Towards the river where the soil is more moist there are a number of maples (*Acer*), planted above all for their autumn colors (*A. Cappadocicum, A. Ginnala, A. Japonicum* 'Vitifolium,' *A. Palmatum* 'Senaki,' *A. Macrophyllum,* A. *Palmatum* 'Dissectum Atropurpureum'). Spring at Ninfa brings into flower many highly scented shrubs such as *Lonicera fragrantissima,* as well as *Viburnum* (*V.* x *Burkwoodii, V.. Farreri, V. Plicatum*). Later in the season ornamental apples, sited on a hillock, come into flower (*Malus floribunda, M. Hupehensis,* 'Profusion'). This elevated position and the wonderful border of color that they form near the little ponds make this one of the most attractive parts of the garden.

Often, alongside the exposed southern side of the ruins, we find *Ceanothus,* their blue color adapting well

Right: The Piazzale della Gloria and lavender avenue against a backdrop of the outer wall showing one of Ninfa's distinctive fortified observation towers.

Opposite: The castle tower, completed in 1300, as seen from the birch grove.

to the soft tint of the stone. Ninfa's stone coloring bears the patina of age. Quarried eight hundred years ago and fashioned by masons, the outside surfaces of the walls take on a wonderful hue. Of the *Ceanothus* the most in evidence are *arboreus* 'Trewithen Blue,' *C. cyaneus*, *foliosus*, 'Gloire de Versailles,' and 'Indigo.'

The ruins provide ideal climbing surfaces for clematis,

which appear all over the garden. Many are large-flower varieties that can be seen from some distance, including *C. armandii*, *C. chrysocoma*, *C. henryi*, 'Lasurstern,' 'Perle d'Azur,' 'President,' and 'Ville de Lyon.'

The river is the life of Ninfa and, though small, it is made more effective by its wooden and stone bridges, pure water, and intense green vegetation and flowering banks. Along with aquatic irises and *Zantedeschia aethiopica* there are great clusters of *Gunnera*

manicata, whose huge leaves can stretch halfway across
the river. Nearer the center of the garden are thriving
plantations of bamboo (*Phyllostachys mitis*), in whose
shade are various ivies and *Acanthus spinosus*. Long
stems of wisteria cross the river, covering whole walls
of the ancient house, including *Wisteria floribunda*
and *sinensis* 'Alba.'

To the west, near the ruined Church of San Biagio,
there is a small hill made from stones brought together
after the outer walls were destroyed. It is known as "the
little hill," and it is here that Donna Lelia created the
rock garden, now one of the most eye-catching features
of Ninfa. Infinite care is required to look after the
hundreds of perennial and rock garden plants, an effort
amply rewarded by the excellent coloring achieved
throughout much of the year.

Roses are everywhere—in the avenues, in trees and hedges, along the river, on gates. Some of them flower until October of each year. Especially worthy of mention from among the huge variety are *banksiae* 'Lutea,' *R. bracteata*, *R. chinensis* 'Mutabilis,' *R. hugonis*, 'Ballerina,' 'Iceberg,' 'Max Graf,' 'Complicata,' 'Penelope,' 'Buff Beauty,' 'Mme Alfred Carrière,' 'Kiftsgate,' and 'Gloire de Dijon.'

Respect for nature's own choices has always been the way of conserving Ninfa's romantic disorder. Spontaneous growth is encouraged—of anemones, cyclamen, daisies, and dandelions. Some of these willingly take root at the very top of certain buildings, such as wild antirrhinums (snapdragon) and cap plants (*Capparis spinosa*). A walk much favored by visitors is the lavender avenue (*Lavandula spica*), which is lined by more than half a mile (more than one kilometre) of lavender hedging. It flowers in June and for two months adds stunningly to the scenic effect.

The mild climate of Ninfa allows tropical plants to prosper, and it is interesting to see the two tall avocado trees in the closed garden created by Francesco Caetani. In this garden, with its recently restored fountains, there is an abundance of fruits, including grapefruit trees (*Citrus maxima*) and, in their shade, raspberries (*Rubus idaeus*).

Opposite: Even this majestic pine is fewer than one hundred years old. *Overleaf*: The Ponte di Legno is one of only four bridges at Ninfa today.

69

Opposite: In early morning the mountain dissolves from view to create a soft, blueish background to pine, cypress, and flowering cherry.

The numerous shrubs at Ninfa are planted not just for their beauty, but also to provide a home for birds and insects. There are many *Buddleia davidii*, which flower beautifully in summer and attract butterflies, and several types of cotoneaster and pyracantha, the vivid winter berries of which provide food for the birds. Bees also have a part in all this, in the pollination of flowers. There are around one hundred bee colonies at Ninfa. From time to time a few will abandon the comfort of their wooden hives and settle in inaccessible places high up in the buildings.

No pesticides are used at Ninfa, and there is little need for them as the earth is healthy. Natural fertilizers are used to strengthen plants and make them resistant to disease. Each gardener at Ninfa is responsible for a specific area, and each prepares the necessary composts.

Care of the ruined buildings and monuments is critical and gardeners carry out minor repairs and other restoration when the garden demands less attention. So important are the ruined walls and buildings, and so integral to the garden, that the role of a "gardener for buildings" has emerged, which in effect means that a member of the garden staff is responsible for the care of those plants, cultivated or native, that flourish among the stones and on the very walls of the ruined buildings.

The Future

The future well-being of Ninfa requires goodwill and common sense. More than these, there must continue to be a profound respect for the Caetani family traditions, and a combination of the sensitive husbandry and conscientious management that have served Ninfa so well.

Ninfa is alive with fresh initiatives designed to strengthen and protect the garden well into the new millennium and to conserve the vision of those who created it. An important element of this is the garden's educational value in nature and the environment. This is given first by example, but increasingly through workshops, study groups, and conferences. Also critical is the goodwill of Ninfa's many friends the world over, as well as an abiding sense of the accountability of future generations.

For the latter, the hardest task may well be that of understanding Ninfa for what it really is; that is to say not just an outstandingly beautiful garden but a retreat.

Opposite: This ruined riverside house was once an anchoring point for rowboats entering Ninfa with fruit and vegetables for sale.

75

an inspiration, a cultural stimulus, and an experience. Painters, musicians, poets, experts in restoration and the environment, great gardeners, members of royal households, statesmen, and students–all these continue to visit Ninfa for the inspiration it provides and the magic that it works in them.

Ninfa is often described as a vision of paradise and, indeed, some of the special places in the garden have names fit for their particular beauty: the biggest open space, with its flowering cherries bursting out in a profusion of color, is the Piazzale della Gloria; the area adjacent to the little Roman bridge is known as the "place of good thoughts"; and the wonderful line of hornbeam near the arboretum, forming a gothic vault nearly two hundred twenty yards (two hundred meters) long, is known as "the cathedral."

Ninfa must not just survive, but must prosper. For that to happen, the very quality of intimacy that draws people to it has to be preserved. When the garden was first conceived, as a family retreat, public visits would have been unimaginable, and yet today Ninfa depends on such visits. Over the years the visiting public have come to appreciate the need to limit garden openings to just a few days a month, and for tours to be accompanied by guides. So far this system of benign control has worked well, preserving Ninfa's unique character and protecting it from physical damage.

With an eye to the future, the wildlife protection area of Ninfa has been dramatically expanded from the original twenty-acre confines of the garden to some thirty-five hundred acres, making it one of the largest and best-known nature preserves in Italy. The thousands of annual visitors, from all over the world, have in turn contributed to the development of a small supplementary economy of significant benefit to the local population.

Foreseeing continued growth in the popularity of the garden and hence in the pressures put upon it, the Fondazione Roffredo Caetani, founded by Donna Lelia to carry on the family's work and traditions after her death, has worked tirelessly in recent years to create a dedicated wildlife park. When complete, this will occupy some two hundred acres adjacent to Ninfa, where many thousands of trees and shrubs have already been planted and where there will eventually be lakes, brooks, and marshes for wildlife. Members of the public will then be able to combine a visit to the park with a visit to the garden, or visit the park independently. In a setting similar to that which would have existed centuries ago, they will be able to enjoy a wonderful variety of wild flowers, migrating birds, and mammals. Another great enterprise will have been completed.

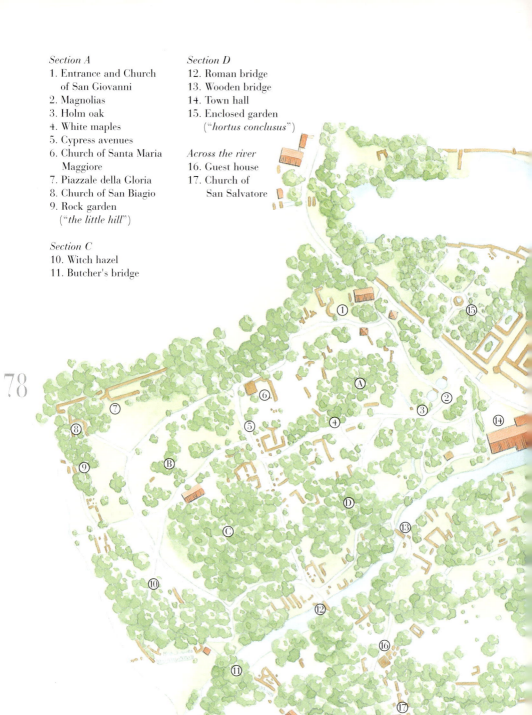

Section A
1. Entrance and Church of San Giovanni
2. Magnolias
3. Holm oak
4. White maples
5. Cypress avenues
6. Church of Santa Maria Maggiore
7. Piazzale della Gloria
8. Church of San Biagio
9. Rock garden ("*the little hill*")

Section C
10. Witch hazel
11. Butcher's bridge

Section D
12. Roman bridge
13. Wooden bridge
14. Town hall
15. Enclosed garden ("*hortus conclusus*")

Across the river
16. Guest house
17. Church of San Salvatore

78

Garden Plan and Visiting Information

Ninfa is open to the public on the first weekend of the month from April to October.

Visiting hours are from 9.00 a.m. to 12 noon, and from 2:30 p.m. to 6:00 p.m.

Special group visits are permitted at special rates subject to demand, but detailed applications must be submitted in writing at least three months prior as follows :
La Direzione
Giardini di Ninfa
04010 Doganella di Ninfa
Latina / Italy
tel: 07 73 69 54 04

All tours are accompanied by a guide, and English is spoken.

Parking and all public conveniences, including light refreshments, are available.

There are conveniently located hotels in Sermoneta (Hotel Principe Serrone, tel: 0773 30342), Norma (Hotel Villa del Cardinale, tel: 0773 354611), and Latina, (Hotel Victoria Palace, tel: 0773 66 3966).

Other interesting local attractions include the medieval castle town of Sermoneta, several thirteenth-century monasteries, and the Circeo National Park.

Directions from Rome: Take the SS Pontina, exit to Cisterna, turn south on the Appia, and after 4 kms take a left turn marked Ninfa.

Ninfa is approximately forty-five miles (seventy kilometers) southeast of Rome, and one hundred ten miles (one hundred seventy kilometers) from Naples.

Page 1: The old-fashioned Bordeaux mixture is the only fungicide in use at Ninfa, giving the trunk of this prunus tree its unusual coloring.

Pages 2-3: Spring coloring against the soft tint of Ninfa's limestone, quarried eight hundred years ago.

Pages 4-5: In early times this little bridge, known as the Ponte Romano, provided an alternative crossing over the River Ninfa when the Via Appia between Naples and Rome flooded.

Page 6: A view across the river from the north bank.

Page 8: Ninfa is famous for its vivid spring blossoms, which can peak as early as March. Abundant water allows plants, which would otherwise not survive the severe summer heat of this region, to be irrigated throughout the year.

First published in the United Kingdom in 1999
by Thames & Hudson Ltd, 181A High Holborn,
London WC1V 7QX

British Library Cataloguing-in-Publication Data
A catalogue record for this book is available
from the British Library

ISBN 0-500-01974-6

Printed and bound in Italy

Series editor Gabrielle Van Zuylen
Designed by Marc Walter / Bela Vista

THE
DESK LAMP

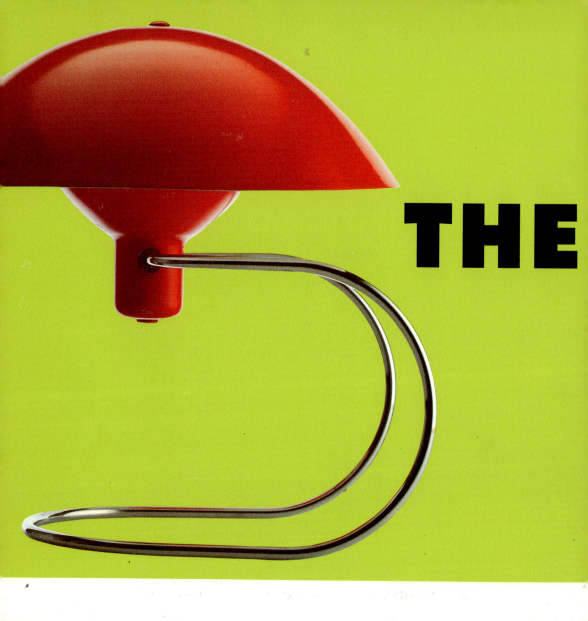

THE

DESK LAMP

AN APPRECIATION

AURUM PRESS

KATE MCINTYRE ◉ PHOTOGRAPHS BY GUY RYECART

First published in Great Britain 1998 by
Aurum Press Limited
25 Bedford Avenue
London WC1B 2AT

A catalogue record for this book is
available from the British Library

ISBN 1 85410 596 5

This book was conceived,
designed and produced by
THE IVY PRESS LIMITED
2/3 St Andrews Place
Lewes, East Sussex
BN7 1UP

Art Director: *Peter Bridgewater*
Editorial Director: *Sophie Collins*
Managing Editor: *Anne Townley*
Project Editor: *Caroline Earle*
Editor: *Julie Whitaker*
Designer: *Ron Bryant-Funnell*
Photography: *Guy Ryecart*

Printed and bound in China

Throughout this book the dimensions of
the objects are given in imperial and
metric measurements; height and width
are expressed by H and W.

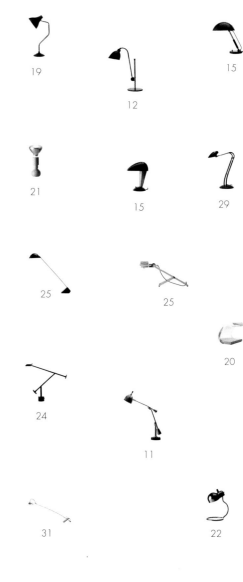

19

12

15

21

15

29

25

25

20

24

11

31

22

30

18

22

16

12

29

19

14

10

17

26

23

16

26

27

21

17

11

30

18

14

13

28

Introduction

'Let there be light.' This phrase from Genesis indicates the basic elemental power of light – a power that transcends cultural barriers. In English the word 'light' has the added meaning of physical weightlessness, suggesting a release from the constraints of the material world. Light is liberation, from darkness and ignorance. With the

Type K, No. 211
Christian Dell, 1974

advent of electricity at the dawning of the 20th century, light was seen at last to be completely within the control of humankind, removing forever the cyclical natural world order of day and night. Electric light is emblematic of modernity – and indeed Modern Movement architects and designers seized upon the new technology with missionary zeal, dreaming up new forms

P H 4-3
Louis Poulsen/Poul Henningsen 1927

that adapted to each rapid advance in lighting technology. Desk lamps produced in the late 1920s by the staff and students of the German design school, the Bauhaus, demonstrate the impact of the new technology on design. Laszlo Moholy Nagy, an artist who experimented with light in his work, shifted the focus of the metal workshop from the production of fine craft objects in precious metals, dubbed 'spiritual samovars and intellectual doorknobs' by one student, to that of light fittings. The philosophy of the

Desk Lamp
Schwinter and Graff
1928

Bauhaus was that good design could transform the consciousness of those who lived with it, and the use of light in the modern interior carried powerful connotations of purity and cleanliness.

In the case of the task lamp these elements combine with the redemptive power of work. The designs from the Bauhaus celebrate the machine aesthetic, using chromium-plated tubular steel, spun aluminium and glass in stark geometric forms. Although the Bauhaus ideal was to design lamps that could be mass produced and therefore benefit as many users as possible, some designs evoked the aesthetic of the machine while defying machine production. In fact Wilhelm Wagenfeld and Carl Jucker's MT10 of 1923–24 can be considered as an early example of the desk lamp as design icon – the symbolism and status

MT10
Wilhelm Wagenfeld and
Carl Jucker
1923–24

**Polaroid No. 114
Executive**
*Polaroid Corp./Walter
Dorwin Teague
1939*

of the design being an inherent part of its function.

This dual function of the task lamp cannot be underestimated. Placed on the desk of the senior executive or the drawing board of the fashionable architect, its purpose is to illuminate effectively while transmitting signals of power, status and artistic credibility. An early example of this is Edouard Buquet's Type A, produced in 1927 and immediately adopted by the Parisian artistic milieu as desk sculpture. The form of the desk lamp acts as an indicator of both contemporary culture and its technology. In their streamlined contours both Walter Dorwin Teague's Executive lamp for Polaroid and the French Jumo lamp celebrate the exhilaration of speed without moving from the desktop. The US mania for UFO-spotting inspired the shapes of the lightshades in desk lamps of the 1950s, and the space race determined the aesthetic of a clutch of plastic desk lamps in the 1960s. Richard Sapper's 1970s' Tizio adopts the form of the oil pump in a decade in which oil prices would dominate the state of the economy.

In contrast with the Modernist 'Form Follows Function' approach to design, Memphis, a group of designers in

Dania
*Artemide/Dario Tognon
1969*

Milan, focused on the cultural significance of artefacts in their designs. The zoomorphic form and primary colours of the Tahiti reassert the element of play and fun that characterized the pop designs of the 1960s, while a lamp by Ettore Sottsass put the architecture of ancient empires on

Tahiti
*Memphis/Ettore Sottsass
1981*

the desks of the captains of industry in the 1980s. As we approach the start of a new millennium the design of the desk lamp reflects the impact of current technologies on our lifestyles. The Nastro reflects the inner workings of the computer – a technological advance that has completely redefined the meaning of 'desktop' – while Philippe Starck's Ara, named after his daughter, encapsulates the merging of the traditionally masculine world of work and the feminine

Don Quixote
Ingo Maurer, 1989

world of the home. Ingo Maurer's Don Quixote fights its way through the banality of the everyday in pursuit of higher ideals, while his lamp designs for the 1990s reflect a return to minimalism and spirituality. Los Minimalos and Mozzkito barely retain a physical presence – the form of the lamp is stripped to the minimum to focus on the metaphysical quality of the light itself – a fourth dimension to usher in the New Age.

NICKEL-PLATED BRASS AND STEEL, GLASS, OPALESCENT GLASS SHADE

1923-4, H17 X W10IN / H43 X W26CM

MT10

WILHELM WAGENFELD
AND CARL JACOB JUCKER

A collaboration between two students at the Dessau Bauhaus, the MT10 was inspired by the work of Laszlo Moholy Nagy. Walter Gropius encouraged the metal workshops to produce designs for industry and a series of prototypes was created for the 1924 Leipzig Fair. This design, however, was commercially unviable and remains an elitist craft object.

PATINATED STEEL,
BAKELITE, FROSTED
GLASS, 1927,
H17.5 X W13IN /
H44 X W32.5CM

NICKEL-PLATED BRASS, ALUMINIUM, LACQUERED
WOOD, LEAD, 1927, H30 X W20IN / H75 X W50CM

P H 4-3

LOUIS POULSEN/
POUL HENNINGSEN

Poul Henningsen's series of lighting
prototypes won all six prizes in a
competition to decide the exhibits for
the Danish Pavilion at the 1925 Paris
Exhibition. By 1927, when this version
was produced, his lighting designs were
internationally recognized and featured
in the Weissenhof Siedlung housing
project in Stuttgart.

TYPE A

W. W. BUQUET/
EDOUARD-WILFRIED
BUQUET

The functional modernism
of this articulated desk
lamp ensured its cult status
among the Parisian Artistes
Décorateurs of the 1920s
and 1930s. Appearing in
smart architects' offices and
interiors and photographed
for the art and architectural
press, it was displayed on
Lucien Rollin's 'Desk of a
Technician' at the Salon
de la Société des Artistes
Décorateurs in 1929.

NICKEL-PLATED BRASS, ALUMINIUM, 1928,
H17 X W10.5IN / H42 X W26.5CM

NICKEL-PLATED BRASS, EBONITE, LACQUERED
SHEET STEEL, LACQUERED STEEL, 1929,
H22 X W8.5IN / H55 X W21.5CM

DESK LAMP

SCHWINTER
AND GRAFF

This simple lamp with adjustable shade was designed by a student at the Bauhaus in Dessau. It was used as a desk lamp by Marianne Brandt, acting head of the metal workshop. In 1928 Marianne Brandt was instrumental in signing a contract with the manufacturers Schwinter and Graff, the producers of this and 52 other Bauhaus designs.

TYPE K, NO. 211

CHR. ZIMMERMANN/
CHRISTIAN DELL

Christian Dell, an experienced silversmith, turned his skills to developing designs for industrial production as craft master at the Bauhaus metal workshop. This task lamp epitomizes his preoccupation with innovation in geometric form, combined with a desire for optimum efficiency, standardization and honest use of materials.

STOVE-LACQUERED

RHOMIUM, 1930.

H33.5 X W7IN /

H84 X W18CM

BESTLITE
BEST AND LLOYD/R. D. BEST

This British classic, designed as a floor lamp in 1930 by Robert Dudley Best, is still in production in a variety of formats. The shade rotates and tilts through its axis, while the arm tilts and rotates through 360 degrees via a 'clutch' mechanism. The Bestlite bears more than a passing resemblance to the Type K.

IDELL 6580 SUPER

GEBR. KAISER & CO./ CHRISTIAN DELL

Christian Dell's double-headed 6580 Super is a development of his Idell 6556 Super. The use of two luminaires and angled tubular steel in the 6580 provides greater flexibility and a much wider spread of light than the single-stemmed version and appears to have been conceived for an office rather than a domestic environment.

ANGLEPOISE

HERBERT TERRY & SONS/ GEORGE CARWARDINE

Patented as the 'Equipoise', the Anglepoise has been in continuous production since 1934, and is a standard fixture in student rooms. Designed by George Carwardine, an engineer specializing in automobile suspension systems, the lamp uses joints based on those of the human arm, offering complete flexibility and balance.

BLACK LACQUERED METAL, REFLECTOR ENAMELLED WHITE INSIDE, 1933–4, H20 X W8IN / H50 X W20CM

ALUMINIUM, STEEL, WOOD AND CAST-IRON, c1934, H16 X W13IN / H40 X W32CM

DESK LAMP

BAUHAUS/KARL TRABER

Traber's desk lamp is a development of the simple designs coming out of the Bauhaus metal workshop in the late 1920s. The articulation of the stem of the lamp is found at its base, increasing both its flexibility and the reach of the light directed onto the work surface.

POLAROID NO. 114 EXECUTIVE

POLAROID CORP. 1939–41/ WALTER DORWIN TEAGUE

Walter Dorwin Teague, together with his son Walter Dorwin Teague Jr. and Frank Del Giudice, carried out a radical redesign of a desk lamp for the Polaroid Corporation. Teague's streamlined design used a light diffuser of polarized cellulose film to reduce eyestrain by eliminating glare. It far outperformed the original in terms of function, price and style.

BAKELITE, ALUMINIUM, PLASTIC, 1939,
H13 X W10IN /
H32.5 X W26CM

H50 (140 MAX) X W19CM / H20 (56 MAX) X W7.5IN, STEEL, 1945, BAKELITE, CHROME-PLATED

LACQUERED METAL AND ALUMINIUM, 1949,
H12 X W26IN / H30 X W65CM

JUMO

ETS. JUMO

The base and shade of the Jumo are made from phenol formaldehyde, a plastic marketed as Bakelite. Closed, the lamp evokes the streamlined forms of American trains and automobiles styled by the Frenchman Raymond Loewy. Open, it resembles a robot or 'Transformer' and has a rather menacing air.

TURBINO

ARREDOLUCE, MONZA/
ACHILLE AND PIERGIACOMO
CASTIGLIONI

The Castiglioni brothers' designs for lighting are driven by advances in technology – the lighting fixture is always subordinate to the lighting effect. The form of the Turbino is determined by the light source, a tubular fluorescent bulb that, though developed in 1939, only became widely available in the postwar period.

LACQUERED METAL, 1950
H18 X W6IN / H45 X W15CM

LACQUERED METAL, 1950s,
H17 X W11.5IN / H42.5 X W29CM

SUN LAMP
NOVELECTRIC/MAX BILL

The symmetric geometry of the Sun Lamp springs from Max Bill's preoccupation with pure form, fostered during his studentship at the Bauhaus. While the shade and the base share a common form, their functions are polarized: that of the base is weighted, static; that of the shade freemoving and flexible.

DESK LAMP
PHILIPS

The disc-shaped shade evokes the obsession with flying saucers that swept the US in the 1950s. This craze spawned a rash of UFO-inspired products, from powder compacts to sherbet sweets. The lamp was manufactured by the Dutch company Philips, who started production of carbon filament lamps in 1891 and who continue to produce innovative lighting to this day.

ANYWHERE

NESSEN LAMPS/
GRETA VON NESSEN

Nessen Studio in New York was set up by Bauhaus-trained designer Walter von Nessen in 1927. After his death, his widow Greta took control of the business, introducing some of her own designs. The Anywhere lamp was selected for the Good Design exhibition at the Museum of Modern Art in New York in 1952.

TABLE LAMP

ARTELUCE/GINO SARFATTI

Gino Sarfatti, founder of Arteluce and an innovative lighting designer in his own right, was a pervasive force in Italian lighting in the 1950s. This lamp shows an obvious debt to the functionalism of Bauhaus tempered with a touch of the contemporary 'cocktail cherry' aesthetic in the exaggeration of the ball and socket mechanism.

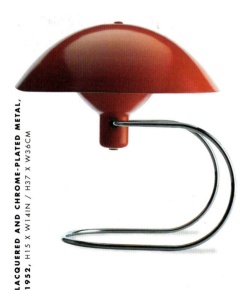

LACQUERED AND CHROME-PLATED METAL, 1952, H15 X W14IN / H37 X W36CM

BRASS, LACQUERED SHEET STEEL, 1952, H16 X W9IN / H40 X W23CM

DESK LAMP

KARL HAGENAUER

The spun aluminium shade of this Austrian lamp resembles those used on the Luxo lamp, a version of the Anglepoise marketed by Jac Jacobsen in the US. The swivel arm, however, breaks completely with both the Anglepoise jointed arm and the rational tubular steel of a generation of Bauhaus-inspired lamps.

DESK LAMP

PHILIPS/LOUIS KALFF

The asymmetry of Kalff's lamp is characteristic of design in the 1950s, from Alexander Calder's mobiles to Carlo Mollino's furniture designs. Although produced in Holland, there are elements of Italian styling in the base, and the dome of the aluminium shade reflects America's obsession with UFOs.

CHROMED METAL, ALUMINIUM AND PLASTIC, 1956, H22 X W11.5IN / H56 X W29CM

LACQUERED ALUMINIUM, BRASS, 1957-59, H16 X 13IN / H40.5 X W32.5CM

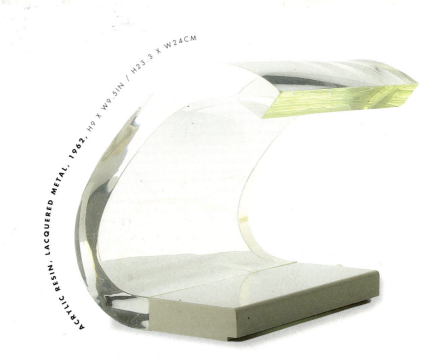

ACRYLIC RESIN, LACQUERED METAL, 1962, H9 X W9.5IN / H23.3 X W24CM

ACRILICA

O-LUCE/JOE COLOMBO

This elegant lamp uses a classic 1960s material – acrylic – in a completely innovative fashion. A light beam is emitted from a bulb in the base and transmitted through to the leading edge of the C-shaped (C for Colombo) Perspex body. The curve at the top of the C directs the light down onto the desk.

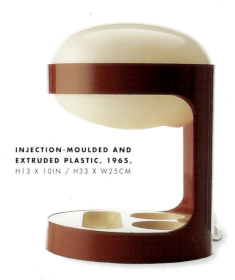

**INJECTION-MOULDED AND
EXTRUDED PLASTIC, 1965,**
H13 X 10IN / H33 X W25CM

KD27

KARTELL/JOE COLOMBO

The KD27 was developed out of Colombo's interest in the use of materials and flexible systems that employed standardized parts in various combinations. The shade is made from injection-moulded plastic and is designed to fit stands cut from extruded-plastic tubing to form a ceiling, table or, in this case, desk lamp with integrated desk tidy.

600

ARTELUCE/GINO SARFATTI

The leatherette beanbag base of this lamp evokes pop artist Claes Oldenburg's 'soft' sculptures and De Pas, D'Urbino and Lomazzi's baseball mitt 'Joe' sofa of 1970, while providing the functional elements of stability and flexibility. It can be either used as a miniature desk lamp or placed on the floor to create ambient lighting.

**LACQUERED METAL, SYNTHETIC
LEATHER, LEAD, 1966,**
H8 X W3IN / H21 X W7CM

LACQUERED ALUMINIUM, 1969, H16 X W13.5IN / H41 X W34CM

DANIA
ARTEMIDE/DARIO TOGNON

The year 1969 saw the US winning the space race with the successful Apollo moon landing. This giant leap for mankind was celebrated in all aspects of design from clothing to domestic appliances. Shaped like an astronaut's helmet, the Dania gives form to an historic moment that captured the popular imagination.

MINITOPO
STILNOVO/JOE COLOMBO

The Topo gains its name from its mouse-like form and reflects Joe Colombo's mission to design flexible systems for living environments unshackled by the traditional preconceptions of the domestic or office interior. This lamp can be configured out of a variety of parts, using a base or clamp to suit specific needs.

CHROME-PLATED METAL, PLASTIC, 1970, H13.5 X W11.5IN / H34 X W29CM

LACQUERED METAL, ABS PLASTIC, 1971, H15.5 X W12IN / H39 X W30.5CM

LAMPIATA

STILNOVO/JONATHAN DE PAS, DONATO D'URBINO, PAOLO LOMAZZI

Italian Radical Design Trio, De Pas, D'Urbino and Lomazzi, experimented with flexibility and interchangeability in their designs for industry. The classic components of a desk lamp have been isolated in the Lampiata, the shade slotting into the weighted base at a choice of angles, without upsetting the equilibrium of the overall design.

H32 X W4.5IN / H80 X W11CM

LACQUERED METAL, PLASTIC, 1972,

TIZIO

ARTEMIDE/RICHARD SAPPER

This high-tech design became a cult object in the 1980s. The weight of the transformer in the base counterbalances the articulated metal arms that conduct power to the bulb without the need for cables. The elegant construction allows this desk light to become a standard lamp at a touch.

SINTESI

ARTEMIDE/
ERNESTO GISMONDI

The synthesis between form and function, aesthetics and technology, is evident in a task lamp that provides both directional and ambient light. The philosophy of its designer Ernesto Gismondi, founder of the Italian lighting company Artemide, is that a lamp should be as aesthetically pleasing switched off as on.

LACQUERED METAL, 1975,
H17 X 5IN / H42 X 13.5CM

IPOTENUSA

FLOS/ACHILLE CASTIGLIONI

The sculptural simplicity of this lamp is a product of the mind of an engineer. Euclidean geometry inspired the rake of the arm of the Ipotenusa: it forms the hypotenuse of a right-angled triangle. The red-tinted skirt of the shade guarantees a perfect pool of light on the desktop.

METAL, ACRYLIC, 1976, H22 X W20IN / H55 X W50CM

METAL, PLASTIC, RUBBER, ELECTRICAL COMPONENTS, 1981, H24 X W9IN / H60 X W22CM

METAL, WOOD, PLASTIC LAMINATE, 1981, H25 X W14.5IN / H63 X W36.5CM

AERIAL LIGHT R S C700
ONE OFF/RON ARAD

In the early 1980s a number of London designer-makers became preoccupied with recycling the debris of escalating consumerism, their collective output tagged 'Creative Salvage'. Ron Arad's Aerial Light, a 'One Off', remote-controlled desk light, is simultaneously an indictment of our remote-control culture and the ultimate executive toy.

TAHITI
MEMPHIS/ETTORE SOTTSASS

The Tahiti was designed in the year that Sottsass founded the design group Memphis, and bears all the traits associated with 'The New International Style'. The form of the desk lamp has been completely reconsidered in an exotic, humorous way. Memphis abandoned the tenets of modernism in favour of a celebration of the ephemeral and the surface.

PIERCED
BLACK METAL
GAUZE,
GLASS, GILT
FINISH
METAL, 1983,
H16 X W18IN /
H39.5 X
W45CM

DESK LAMP
ARTEMIDE/ETTORE SOTTSASS

The desk lamp as Greek temple. The tectonic forms of this lamp are evidence of Sottsass's initial training as an architect and his fascination with the architecture and culture of Ancient Greece. He considers that 20th-century objects should be imbued with the mystic qualities of ancient ritual implements.

METAL, PLASTIC, 1983-4, H18 X W24IN / H45.5 X W60CM

NASTRO

STILNOVO/ALBERTO FRASER

Consultant designer Alberto Fraser was inspired to create this lamp by the maze of coloured plastic wire to be found inside the rationalized outer casings of computers. The name Nastro (Italian for ribbon) comes from this computer 'ribbon'. The multi-coloured extruded-plastic arm combines decoration with function; it houses the electrical wiring, is fully flexible and will retain any given position.

CHROME-PLATED METAL, 1988,
H22.5 X W7IN / H56.6 X W17.5CM

ARA
FLOS/PHILIPPE STARCK

Philippe Starck predicted that the days of the office were numbered. His design for a desk lamp fulfils his desire to provide perfect tools for transitional environments – living spaces as work spaces, and vice versa. By naming all his designs – Ara is named after his daughter – Starck tempers the anonymity of the mass-produced product.

TANGO
ARTELUCE/STEPHAN COPELAND

The movement of Copeland's lamp design is expressive of the sensuality of the tango. The anthropomorphic element is reinforced by the use of two 'legs' rather than the conventional single stem of most desk lamps. Combined with the ribbed green shade, the overall effect is aggressive – desk lamp as velociraptor?

CHROME-PLATED METAL, 1989,
H44 X W9.5IN / H110 X W24CM

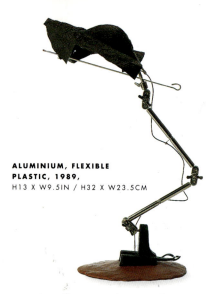

ALUMINIUM, FLEXIBLE
PLASTIC, 1989,
H13 X W9.5IN / H32 X W23.5CM

STAINLESS STEEL,
SPUN STEEL AND
ALUMINIUM, 1994,
H25 X W6IN / H62 X W15CM

DON QUIXOTE
INGO MAURER

Here is a lamp that is less concerned with the material world than the pursuit of lofty, if unattainable, ideals. Named after Cervantes' enthusiastic visionary, the Don Quixote jousts at the invisible windmills on your desk. Its 'Touch-tronic' switch responds instantly to more mundane requirements – tapped once, the lamp switches on, longer contact dims the light.

LOS MINIMALOS UNO
INGO MAURER /
INGO MAURER AND TEAM

Philosophy and state-of-the-art technology combine again in another lamp, this time by Ingo Maurer's design team. While acknowledging the fact that we are all individuals with many facets, Maurer returns to minimalism as the ultimate solution to address our myriad needs and desires – 'The detail makes a product.'

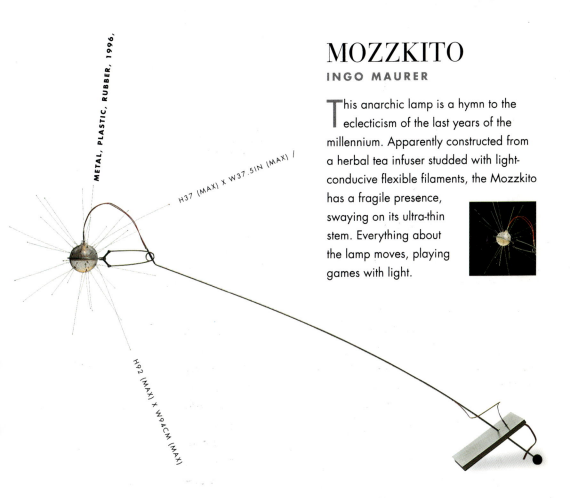

METAL, PLASTIC, RUBBER, 1996,

H37 (MAX) X W37.5IN (MAX) /

H92 (MAX) X W94CM (MAX)

MOZZKITO
INGO MAURER

This anarchic lamp is a hymn to the eclecticism of the last years of the millennium. Apparently constructed from a herbal tea infuser studded with light-conducive flexible filaments, the Mozzkito has a fragile presence, swaying on its ultra-thin stem. Everything about the lamp moves, playing games with light.

ACKNOWLEDGEMENTS

The publishers would particularly like to
thank the following for loan of desk lamps:

Bonhams, London: 17 (left), 19, 22
(right), 23, 27, 28, 32

Catalytico: 30 (right)

Designer Light Shop:
25 (right), 29, 31

Andrew Dunlop: 13

**Vitra Design Museum, Weil-am-
Rhein, Germany:** 1, 2, 6, 7, 8, 9, 10,
11, 12, 14, 15, 16, 17 (right), 18, 20, 21,
22 (left), 24, 25 (left), 26, 30 (left)

Special thanks to
**James McFarlane at Designer Light
Shop, Alexander Payne at
Bonhams, Serge Mauduit at Vitra,
and Andrew Dunlop**

Endpapers:
**Sketch of the Topo lamp
by Joe Colombo**

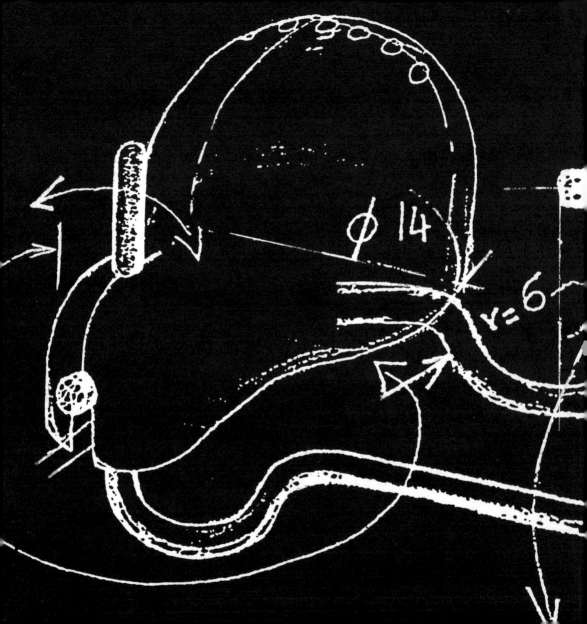